H.E.A.R.

A STARTING POINT FOR DISCIPLESHIP IN A LOUD WORLD

CHRIS LOVELACE

FOREWORD BY JON FIELD

ISBN 978-1-105-01388-1 (First Edition, Paperback)

For questions, requests, and more, contact:

chrislovelace58@yahoo.com
(916) 572-7170

Twitter: @chrislovelace58

TABLE OF CONTENTS

It is an amazing and precious gift to be a part of someone's life.

I am so grateful for my loving wife Denise, my daughters Christina, Camila, Casey, and my son Chris.

A special thank you to my mentor, pastors, and friends on this journey with me. #convergefam #gracefam

I love you.

- Chris Lovelace

FOREWORD

Multiplication. Something we need to always have on our minds as the people of God. It is one thing to share the Gospel of Jesus Christ, it is another to raise up a disciple that shares it.

The Apostle Paul states in 2 Timothy 2:2 that Timothy's assignment was to "teach these truths to other trustworthy people who will be able to pass them on to others." (NLT) This passage forever altered how I view the art of making disciples and my role as a pastor in the process. I want to see every follower of Christ be an effective disciple-maker.

We were talking one day about how many great Bible studies and resources there are for people to grow in their faith. We needed something simple, biblical, and easily repeatable to help people have transformational conversations with others about what they are learning in God's word and in their journey with Christ.

Serving as the District Church Planting Director for our movement of churches called Converge, and as the Discipleship Pastor at Grace Church, Chris has always been passionate about reaching people for Christ and helping them grow.

H.E.A.R. is the culmination of a season where Chris took the time to study different discipleship methods, dig into the Bible, and seek God's heart in the area of Christ-centered discipleship. I distinctly remember the day that he walked into my office full of excitement and began to share the heart behind what you will discover in this book. We have used this tool with ministry leaders, long-time church members, and brand new Christ-followers and have seen life-change happen for the glory of God.

In the pages ahead, you will be taken on the exciting journey of learning how to H.E.A.R. one another and become devoted followers of Christ. I pray you will find what we have discovered that anyone can H.E.A.R. another person and experience the joy of making disciples.

— JON FIELD, LEAD PASTOR OF GRACE CHURCH

H.E.A.R.

A STARTING POINT FOR DISCIPLESHIP IN A LOUD WORLD

INTRODUCTION

*² You have heard me teach things that have been confirmed by many re-
liable witnesses. Now teach these truths to other trustworthy people who
will be able to pass them on to others.*

- 2 Timothy 2:2 (NIV)

We talk a lot.

I mean that as a society, in the 21st century— we talk a lot. We
have audiences of our friends, family, and total strangers in our pock-
ets. We can shout into the void and it all moves at breakneck speed as
everyone tries to get something out there. We can send text messages to
anyone essentially no matter where they are or what time it is. No one
is unreachable, for better or for worse— and that's led us to do a lot of,
well, talking.

All of this talking makes so many people surprisingly lonely. We
can know a lot about each other and not really know a thing. It's not
surprising that we're conditioned to listen passively because of this—
processing our response instead of listening. It's more important now
than ever for us to remember that real listening takes real time, energy,
and action. If there's one thing that God has taught me over the years,
honestly, it's *shut up, Chris!*

I think it's an appropriate place to start, so I'm going to pass that
message on to you. From the most loving place, I truly mean, it's time to
shut up.

The Bible talks a lot about the importance of listening versus
speaking. The word 'hear' appears over 471 times, and 'talk' only 34.
There's a Jewish prayer called the Shema (pronounced shuh-MAH),
which can be found in Deuteronomy 6:4-5. "Hear O Israel, the Lord is
our God, the Lord is one, and as for you, you shall love the Lord your
God with all of your heart, with all your soul, and with all your strength."

The Hebrew word "shema" literally means to hear, שְׁמַע. It's found many times throughout the Bible, describing hearing as a diligent action. It has a broader definition than we have in English— it can be used to mean pay attention, focus, and respond.

God speaks. We listen. The word shema is the name given to the prayer indicated in Deuteronomy which can be interpreted as learning to listen to and love God. When we truly listen, we don't just let the words pass through our ear canals but we rather do the literal action of processing what is spoken. This word is used in the Psalms, when asking for the Lord to listen, and it's also used when God calls for Israel to hear in Exodus. God equates listening in this way with keeping the covenant. It seems obvious when written out this way, but it's always refreshing to me to see the words: listening is obedience. Children listen to their parents and obey. Workers listen to their bosses and obey. When we really listen to God, we obey. As Christians, we should rethink what it truly means for us to hear. Especially in our relationship with God and others.

Hearing should be a foundational part of our Christian walk. God wants us to hear him, and our neighbors want us to hear them. This world is filled up with so much information, chatter, conspiracy theories, and opinions. God wants to speak to us through the noise, and we need to be quick to hear and slow to speak. "People don't care how much you know until they know how much you care." That's a quote actually attributed to President Theodore Roosevelt, but it rings true of all leadership. As those that have been given the work of reconciliation, we must get better at listening.

H.E.A.R. is not about having all the answers, but rather having an easy and effective starting point of discipleship centered on first listening to God and then others. Each letter stands for a full point:

H — His Word: What's God saying to you in His Word?
E — Engage: Who are you engaging with your time, treasure, and talents?
A — Authentic: What's an authentic struggle and success in your faith walk.
R — Reach: Who or where do you want to reach?

These questions are formed from extended research, and prayer of what marks maturity in a disciple. This is not an end-all but a starting point to help guide you. This can be done alone in a devotion time and with others in one on one discipleship. H.E.A.R. is all about starting with these four questions to open up a world of healthy, meaningful connection that presses us deeper in our maturity and accountability as followers of Jesus. These questions are the small first steps that we can ask our church leaders, congregations, neighbors, friends, and loved ones.

Let me reemphasize: it's all about the small steps to make a larger change. It's an old truth in a new light. All we have to do is hear!

H.E.A.R. is not about judgment or offering your personal solutions to problems, it's not about knowing exactly the right thing to say or advice to offer. It's not about you at all. It's about focusing on God and the person in front of you. You'll be glad to know that you won't need a Bible college degree or an outgoing personality either! Instead, it's about effectively putting in effort to decrease your inner thoughts and solutions by listening. We are all called to make disciples, and to raise up disciples that will do the same. By asking these four open-ended key discipleship questions and simply (well, maybe not so simple, but we'll get to that) listening, we can all start on the journey of discipleship that many of us have not had yet or felt under-equipped to have.

This method is most impactful when used in your personal devotional time and one-on-one time with a disciple. A scriptural study should be the primary resource; H.E.A.R. should complement what you are already studying, learning, and sharing with people, not take away from it nor be a substitute for it. The H.E.A.R. starting point of discipleship will add a layer of accountability to teachings, trainings, and relationships. Another thing I love about this is how versatile it is: you can use it in meetings, small groups, leadership training, coffee shops, the hallway in your church or even in your home. The beauty of it is that you don't need to ask all four questions at the same time. Ask a question and let God direct the conversation. I have learned that over time, that when we are consistent with using H.E.A.R. with pastors, leaders, volunteers, and congregation members, they will begin to share the answers to these four questions naturally. They will also begin asking them naturally as well. This begins a culture of mutual accountability!

I'm really glad you picked up this book, whether you've heard of the H.E.A.R. method or if this is the first time you're are seeing it. I have seen many disciples grow and make new disciples committing to these starting point questions. I pray that you will be encouraged by this simple and effective starting point of discipleship as you love God and others!

H: HIS WORD

THE ROAD TO EMMAUS

²⁵ And then He said to them, "You foolish men and slow of heart to believe in all that the prophets have spoken! ²⁶ Was it not necessary for the Christ to suffer these things and to come into His glory?" ²⁷ Then beginning with Moses and with all the Prophets, He explained to them the things written about Himself in all the Scriptures...

..."Were our hearts not burning within us when He was speaking to us on the road, while He was explaining the Scriptures to us?" ³³ And they got up that very hour and returned to Jerusalem, and found the eleven gathered together and those who were with them, ³⁴ saying, "The Lord has really risen and has appeared to Simon!" ³⁵ They began to relate their experiences on the road, and how He was recognized by them at the breaking of the bread.

- Luke 24:13-27, 32b-35 (NASB)

Amazing! I could go on for years about everything happening in that passage of scripture.

If you skimmed over it here because you're already familiar with it and wanted me to get on with it (it's okay, I've done it too), go back and read it. Take in every word. I'll wait.

I will try to keep this chapter as short as possible because it's really important to me to keep this as short and as simple as possible. This is not a formula, but it is just about the principle of accountability and the independent pursuit of Godliness. The first letter in the acronym stands for His Word: a foundational element of discipleship and a significant way God chooses to present Himself.

Now, back to the road: this passage is often talked about in the lens of the resurrection (this is one of the first appearances that He chooses to make, on the third Day after the crucifixion), but I want to focus on a few statements in particular.

25 And then He said to them, "You foolish men and slow of heart to believe in all that the prophets have spoken! 26 Was it not necessary for the Christ to suffer these things and to come into His glory?" 27 Then beginning with Moses and with all the Prophets, He explained to them the things written about Himself in all the Scriptures.

- Luke 24:25-27 (NASB)

The disciples don't yet believe the testimonies they have heard from the women outside the tomb and Jesus lets them know that their faithlessness is noticeable in their scriptural ignorance of the truth. Essentially, He reproves them for not having read and truly listened to the Word of God and begins to explain everything about Himself that's written.

Every element of the H.E.A.R. starting point method of of discipleship can't work without the other, but knowing His Word and understanding its uses is absolutely essential to not only the method, but the entire act of discipleship.

First, let's take a look at some applications of God's word.

16 All Scripture is inspired by God and beneficial for teaching, for rebuke, for correction, for training in righteousness; 17 so that the man or woman of God may be fully capable, equipped for every good work.

- 2 Timothy 3:16 (NASB)

God chose to reveal Himself through Scripture, and He chose to do that for us. The Holy Spirit inspired the human authors of the Bible, so we know that it is unchanging inerrant truth.

142 Your righteousness is an everlasting righteousness, and Your law is truth.

- Psalm 119:142 (NASB)

The Word of God declares and commands what is right. He preserves His Word in a recorded format, the Holy Bible, providing to us

what is good, acceptable, holy, and pleasing to him. That's an important thing to remember as you're discipling: the things that God does
for us, through His Word, He enables us to do for others through Him.
A branch produces a flower, which produces a fruit, which produces a
seed, which produces a branch.

Stay tuned for more great plant metaphors. They're Scriptural!

FOR TEACHING

God uses Scripture to teach us and show us the paths of life
that He has designed. Some people refer to this simply as His will. If we
want to see His will, look in His word. God has given us his presence in
recorded form, so any question to life can be found in the Bible. There
is no end to what we can learn through God's word, either. It doesn't
matter if we've been a Christian for eight days, eight weeks, or eighty
years, the Bible is an endless well and we are blessed to drink from it as
often as we need.

Something so beautiful about the Bible and understanding His
Word is that God's intervention is necessary, as 1 Corinthians 2:14-16
says:

*14 But a natural person does not accept the things of the Spirit of God,
for they are foolishness to him; and he cannot understand them, because
they are spiritually discerned. 15 But the one who is spiritual discerns
all things, yet he himself is discerned by no one. 16 For who has known
the mind of the Lord, that he will instruct Him? But we have the mind of
Christ.*

- 1 Corinthians 2:14-16 (NASB)

There is no way we can in one lifetime know or fully understand everything that has been laid out in Scripture. While teachers and
preachers are called to faithfully hear from God, surviving only on a
weekly snack will leave us malnourished. Every Christian should have
a consistent daily diet rich with truth in love found in His Word. God
desires to speak to us everyday right off the pages of the Bible. We are
called to a life of learning, growing, and hearing everyday! The great
news is that God is there every step of the way bringing us strength,

hope, joy, wisdom, safety, and redemption.

God is so good.

FOR REBUKE/CORRECTION

I was on my way home recently from a meeting out of town and right after setting up the directions to my house on my phone, I lost service. The GPS couldn't track where I was, and I got this gentle (but constant) reminder that it was working itself out.

You know the one.

"Recalculating," it chirped every so often.

I was starting to get frustrated as I tried to maneuver myself through the unfamiliar way. Suddenly, it clicked into place and before I knew it, I was back on track. This time, it was a minor inconvenience, it didn't cause me any great distress or anger, but it still was relieving once I knew where I was going (or at least trusting the app to get me home).

God's correction through the Bible is like a recalculation reminder. It's not coming through raising an angry voice or lightning bolts. Scriptural correction is a gentle but clear and firm redirection. It's how God often brings us back, even when we don't know we're going the wrong way. Sometimes we'll land on a particular text and be surprised at how we're drifting away. That's God's realignment, using His word as a guide. That's why each day it is important we hear from Him. It is not condemnation. Condemnation is from the enemy. God sanctifies us in His truth and if we remain diligent to hear his correction, he provides unshakable council and direction.

God is so good.

FOR TRAINING IN RIGHTEOUSNESS

To revisit the eternal nature of studying the Bible: we can, and should, be learning for our entire lives. Spiritual maturity isn't something achieved in a day. The process of sanctification (the lifelong process of becoming more like Jesus) is not quick and it's not easy. Scripture should be used as a trainer in forming spiritually healthy habits. This is God telling us that we will be taught lessons over and over again, and the only way we can do this is by frequenting and cherishing His Word.

² but whose delight is in the law of the Lord,
    and who meditates on his law day and night.
³ That person is like a tree planted by streams of water,
    which yields its fruit in season
and whose leaf does not wither—
    whatever they do prospers.

- Psalm 1:2-3 (NIV)

Some of the lessons we'll learn in brokenness. Some from the top of the world. Some we'll learn when we think we don't need them, others when we are actively seeking out answers. We'll learn some quickly and some very slowly. Some we will learn surrounded with support. Still others we will learn with only ourselves and God.

This use of His Word is especially valuable when we are discipling others. Psalm 1:3 describes the person whose delight is in the Word of God as a "tree planted by streams of water." This tree is flourishing because of its approximation to the waters, which give it what it needs to produce fruit. If God's law and the Holy Spirit is the water and we are the tree, this is yet another Scriptural example of the importance of remaining in our Bibles for instruction. To train in righteousness so we can bear the fruits for the Kingdom of God.

Its leaf does not wither. Whatever they do prospers.

God is so good.

Now that we've taken a brief look at some of the applications of Scripture and what that means for us as individuals, let's go more micro and look at it through the lens of the H.E.A.R. Method and what His Word means in your discipling.

It really can be summed up in one word: **accountability**.

It's important to have accountability for yourself and for the person you're discipling. I mean that in the sense of independence in your study. When using this in one-on-one discipleship, this should point the student of scripture back to their Bible, back to their devotion or reading plan, making sure they are feeding themselves: healthy disciples are always interacting with and wrestling with Scripture. We have to own our faith for ourselves. We can't survive off the faith of others. God's word is where everything starts, and that's the only way for us to survive having our own faith. It points back to Matthew 6:33:

33 But seek first His kingdom and His righteousness, and all these things will be provided to you.

- Matthew 6:33 (NASB)

We need to seek His kingdom above all else. As you guide others in the path of faith, make sure that your student is pointing back to what they are hearing in God's Word first rather than what they heard from you, a commentary, social media, favorite preacher, or a search on the internet.

YOU MIGHT ASK:
What's God saying to you in *His Word*?

The person you're discipling shouldn't feel like you are quizzing them either. You should be asking with genuine interest. With this framework set, they won't feel pressured to be reading scripture, they should *want* to for a number of reasons: one of those being the mutual encouragement it can offer. The goal is for the disciple to be building up habits of inviting God into the reading of His Word with them: training in righteousness, if you will, to in turn expect to share that with others in this environment of discipleship.

Accountability and humility can be hard things to love, but I've really learned to love them because those qualities have to be present for real raw, honest learning. When you're humble, you're willing to be accountable. You're also willing to admit what you don't know and invite God with humility into your readings and teachings to aid in the understanding of the scriptures.

[6] *"God is opposed to the proud, but gives grace to the humble."*
- James 4:6 (NASB)

God has given us food. We need to be hungry for it and ask for his wisdom in humility about what he wants to speak to us about.

Keep your heart and mind open and humble to learn from the person you're discipling, as well. Don't expect for every comment to be on par with the scriptural context of a passage, or for complete exegesis of the text. God doesn't teach by different grade levels. Many people do not know the Bible, and it's not for lack of teachers or preachers. While certainly some church leaders share a portion of the blame for not preaching deeper scripture, there's a large part of personal accountability that comes into play. When asking this question, have an open heart to listen first without interrupting. Always remember the first time you began reading the Bible. I believe a posture of listening to what God is saying to the disciple in His Word is a key ingredient that will encourage the habit of further reading and sharing. Remember, you will have a turn to share with the disciple what you are hearing as well.

This element, His Word, encourages the disciple to keep a high view of Scripture. If someone can't remember what God spoke to them about in their morning devotion, then they are going through the motions instead of hearing what God wants to speak to them about. Discipleship is becoming more and more like Christ. It's too easy to read in the morning, forget, and then go live like the world for the rest of the day. The student should be on high alert for what God is saying. You should ask yourself:

- Do I have accountability?
- Am I self-feeding?
- Am I encouraging you (the disciple) to remember your devotion?

[28] *But He said, "On the contrary, blessed are those who hear the word of God and follow it."*
- Luke 11:28 (NIV)

You will know that the discipleship relationship is gaining strength when you ask the question, and the disciple is excited to answer!

- 23 -

Remind the student to listen closely to Jesus in prayer. When you are deeply rooted, like a tree by a stream, the leaf will not wither. This will be crucial as we look at the next part of the acronym: Engage. You can't effectively engage with others if the Lord isn't talking to you.

OTHER PASSAGES:

- Romans 10:17
- Revelation 1:3
- Luke 18:9-14
- John 15
- Psalm 46
- Psalm 81:8

E: ENGAGE

28 Just as the Son of Man did not come to be served, but to serve, and to give his life as a ransom for many.

- Matthew 20:28 (NIV)

It is such a privilege to wash someone's feet.

If you've ever had the opportunity, you know it's a humbling and honoring experience for both people involved. But we can probably stop pretending it's a super romantic or desirable task: if it were, then it wouldn't be the example of deep servanthood that Jesus set. As a young 32-year-old, wide-eyed and excited church-planting pastor, we decided to hold a foot-washing service to bless and honor the leaders that had completed our leadership training class. I was washing someone's feet, and I remember that day vividly for many reasons: one of which being I don't like feet as I barely look at my own feet, let alone someone else's. I remember taking the socks off of my 6-foot-3 friend... I don't think he really was a foot person either. I mean, he knew that they would be having their feet washed and still chose to wear new black socks. You know what happens when you wear dark socks with shoes and they're new, you get those little pieces of lint sticking to your feet. I'll be honest, to truly understate it, it really wasn't the most pleasant experience I've ever had! But I wanted to make sure that their feet were clean. At that moment, as I was scrubbing those revolting little lint balls out from between their toes, I was reminded of what an amazing example Jesus set for us all.

He washed the disciples' feet after they had walked for miles in sandals. Surely dirt, mud, calluses, even animal feces covered their feet. It was a worshipful moment for so many reasons but something else really struck me then. I could not help but weep at the thought that lint balls were barely a drop in the bucket of what our Lord did.

Jesus washed the feet of his disciples, including Judas'.

He didn't just come to serve those who liked him or followed him. He knew Judas would betray him and he washed his feet anyway. He came to serve and set an example of a servant that doesn't just engage those who encourage or celebrate him only. He came to serve even the ones who would turn their backs on him.

When discipling someone, you're directly engaging them with the resources you have been blessed with, a worshipful act. We are empowered by the Holy Spirit at work in us to engage people on a different level than we could ever do on our own with our time, treasure, and talents. Asking and training up the disciple in the engagement of others functions in a few ways: it's accountability for them to be actively using their faith in their day-to-day lives, it's training in developing and maintaining strong spiritual relationships, and it's an encouraging reminder that their work is valuable to the Kingdom of God.

YOU MIGHT ASK:
Who are you *engaging* with your time, treasure, and talents?

¹²*Very truly I tell you, whoever believes in me will do the works I have been doing, and they will do even greater things than these, because I am going to the Father.*
¹³ *And I will do whatever you ask in my name, so that the Father may be glorified in the Son.* ¹⁴ *You may ask me for anything in my name, and I will do it.*

- John 14:12-14 (NIV)

Jesus gave everything for us. It's humbling to read/see/hear every time, isn't it? He came down in human form, experienced all of the limitations of humanity that we can't even begin to understand, spent

His life in ministry, suffered and was killed in a humiliating, disturbing way. And He considered it an act of service. He gave an example of servanthood throughout His entire ministry. Washing feet, an important example, is still just washing feet. He's calling us to be willing to serve Him by serving others and to care so much, we would die for it.

^{15} If you love Me, you will keep My commandments.
- John 14:15 (NASB)

But He very clearly calls us to model after him in engaging others:

^{37} Jesus replied: "'Love the Lord your God with all your heart and with all your soul and with all your mind.' ^{38} This is the first and greatest commandment. ^{39} And the second is like it: 'Love your neighbor as yourself.' ^{40} All the Law and the Prophets hang on these two commandments."
- Matthew 22:37-40 (NIV)

This question is not formulated from a works based salvation, this is a reflection question to a heart's priorities when we have been saved by the life giving transformation of our salvation. There's no doubt where Jesus asks for our priorities to be. God's heart is for the lost (see Luke 15). I like to divide it into the aforementioned time, treasure, and talents; it makes both personal accountability and discipleship easier to understand when it comes to engaging those around us. The disciple is free to answer on any or all of the Engagement areas.

TIME

Time is the most unique resource that God gives us. We know that every moment we have in our lives is because He has a purpose for it: there's no second that God can't use. It's the only thing we can't get back. It's something we all universally look back on and look forward to. It's separated from everything else that we "own" because there is not a person on earth with control over it. What we do with our time absolutely matters. It's a big deal.

A big 21st century excuse is that we just don't have enough time. As a society, we are technically busy. Communication is faster than ever and technology is rapidly improving, changing the spheres of how we work and play. As more things demand our time and attention, it becomes more and more important that we are prioritizing correctly. It's not a valid excuse to say you didn't have time to engage others in Christ. There are only 24 hours in a day which is the same for everybody and others are finding time to fellowship and participate in Godly activities. How you spend it matters! Time is a valuable commodity and to trust God with it is to know that even the hours spent wondering are purposeful.

Who really has no time? It was the prayer of Moses that reminds us that how we spend our time matters:

[12] *Teach us to number our days that we may get a heart of wisdom.*
- Psalms 90:12 (NIV)

If you're regularly discipling somebody, you're giving your time to Kingdom work. By asking the disciple who they are engaging with their time, it encourages them to actively seek out someone and put their faith into practice by giving time out of their life as a blessing to others. How are you engaging others with your time?

TREASURE

The Bible refers to treasure as things we value, tangible and intangible. There are two major factors in this: possessions and finances. Just to be clear, I'm talking about what the Lord has given us stewardship over, but I think it's important to look back at Matthew 6:

[19] *Do not store up for yourselves treasures on earth, where moths and vermin destroy, and where thieves break in and steal.* [20] *But store up for yourselves treasures in heaven, where moths and vermin do not destroy, and where thieves do not break in and steal.* [21] *For where your treasure is, there your heart will be also.*
- Matthew 6:19-21 (NIV)

The Bible calls us to not hold the treasures we have on earth higher than heavenly treasure, since all of our earthly possessions will be gone eventually and our hearts will follow what we cherish. In 2017, the Sonoma Complex Fires saw over 100,000 people in Santa Rosa evacuated as 5,300 homes lit on fire from the blaze. One of those homes belonged to good friends of mine, Mike and Zoe Baker. Mike shared with me that after the fires had been put out, he took his family back over to the house to view the damage and to salvage anything of value from the property. While there, staring at the pile of ashes and burnt wood that used to be a premiere property, his daughter looked up at him and said "Dad, this is why we store our treasures up in heaven." Over the next few years, I watched as their family joyfully continued to serve the Lord with what little they had left. Her words are a stark reminder that everything here is temporary.

The earthly things of value, our possessions and our finances, have no meaning in eternity unless we dedicate them to God for his purposes rather than simply fulfilling our personal human satisfaction. Plain and simple, it all belongs to God.

Jesus calls for the rich man to leave everything behind and follow Him. Jesus knew that the rich young ruler placed a higher value on those securities rather than Him. God calls us to follow Him and use our treasures for His kingdom. When asking your disciple about use of their treasure, the goal is to get a response that reflects both generosity and humility. This could range from donations to the church, missions, outreach, to the use of their property for a Bible study. The key here is being generous with the earthly treasures God has blessed them with. How are you using your treasures on earth to invest in life change?

TALENTS

I'm using the word talent to describe the unique gifts that each of us have been blessed with to serve.

10 As each has received a gift, use it to serve one another, as good stewards of God's varied grace.

- 1 Peter 4:10 (ESV)

The gifts we've been given are not ours to keep: God intends for us to use them to love others and engage them in spiritual connection. Also, these talents should be traits we are developing constantly. The Holy Spirit works within us to accentuate and accelerate our talents further than we could ever by ourselves. Asking the disciple to examine their own gifts helps encourage them to identify the talents God has given them, invite Him into their personal development, and use them as the hands and feet of Christ. We are to use our talents for the building up of the Church. The talents we have been given allow us to live out and accomplish God's plans for our lives. Using our talents to build up the body of Christ is God's desire for his people. 1 Corinthians 12:8-10 gives us some great examples of these talents to use. We know that it is God's desire that we are displaying his fruit in our lives when we use our talents to serve and build up the church and multiply disciples! What is your gift?

More often than not, these three things (time, treasure, and talent) align! It also doesn't have to be an exclusively Christian environment for a disciple to engage others. Community projects and teams are also a great way for our talents to be used by God to engage others. It also could be as simple as starting a conversation and buying coffee for the person behind you in line or starting a Bible study with your neighbors.

The roots of engagement of others for Jesus are generosity and humility. These areas reflect selfless character in a disciple and critical to our growth. To serve like Jesus should be something all disciples aspire to, and Jesus never lived within the bounds of selfishness and pride. Asking this question helps to remove us from focusing on self. It allows the student to reflect on how they utilize and trust God with their gifting. It places our lives in the context of serving others. It's also a great opportunity for the disciple to be encouraged by the big and small things that God is doing in and through them!

Find time to celebrate how the disciple is glorifying God in accomplishing his work no matter how minimal. Also remember to celebrate how God is using you uniquely to see Kingdom fruit produced!

You should ask yourself:

- What are my unique gifts, talents, and abilities?
- What would I hear from Jesus about my use of them?
- What opportunities are present today where God can use my time, treasure, and talents to be used for his glory?

The next part of the acronym is crucial to engaging as well: public perception widely finds Christian accounts to be lacking in authenticity. Engaging with others means being honest and genuine, truly authentic in loving and serving.

A: AUTHENTICITY

²⁴ And let us consider how to stir up one another to love and good works, ²⁵ not neglecting to meet together, as is the habit of some, but encouraging one another, and all the more as you see the Day drawing near.
- Hebrews 10:24-25 (ESV)

A common negative perception of the modern American church is fueled by mistrust. I hear too often stories of people who avoid church because they've been hurt by hypocrisy or shortcomings in relationships. It's heartbreaking and particularly stunning since the Bible gives us such concrete examples of how to avoid exactly that.

One early summer afternoon when my son Chris was six, he and I went out to an abandoned golf course in California to ride our bikes. If you haven't been to an abandoned golf course to ride a bike, you're really missing out! We rode around the extended paved areas around the course. As we rode around, he spotted a big hill he wanted us to ride down. When we got to the top of the hill, I asked him if he was scared. He insisted he wasn't. I could tell that he hesitated on his answer a bit, so I decided to head down the hill first. As I looked back to check on his reaction to me going down, I was shocked to see him right behind me! As he got to the bottom of the hill, his front wheel wobbled, and he lost control. He landed in a bed of weeds and thorns. As any father would, I quickly asked him if he was alright. He did not want me to see that he was injured, so he got up from the ground and began to walk around in circles, shaking his arms. I asked him again if he was alright, and then he showed me his arms. They had several needles from the thorns that needed to be picked out. He winced in pain with each one of the thorns we removed, one by one, from his arms. When I finally got all of the thorns out, I noticed that he hid an area on his wrist from me. I asked him what he was hiding.

"Nothing." I asked him again, and he said, "It's no big deal, Dad." I finally did what any parent would do— I told him that it would stay in his wrist forever if he didn't let me see. He then proceeded to tell me, "It's okay, dad, won't Jesus give us new bodies in heaven?" I was impressed by his response, but shortly after saying this, he began to cry because the pain was getting intense. He flipped over his wrist to show me that there was one last thorn remaining. A thorn I did not know about. One he was hiding using his other hand. It was a thorn stuck deep in the sensitive crease area in his wrist, right below the palm. It was red and swelling. He knew it would hurt to take it out, but it would hurt more to keep it in. I encouraged him to let me get it out. We did, and we went back out to ride again!

If we only removed the parts of the splinters we could see, the parts of the splinters that are below the surface would get infected. God wants to handle the larger authentic areas that are deeper underneath the surface.

Being authentic is a critical core part of healthy discipleship relationships. The only way that real authentic dialogue happens is when we are humble. The Bible gives us plenty of great direction and examples of this, particularly that of the apostle Paul. In the Corinthians, Paul shares a lot about why he is proud of the church and happy to have been their spiritual father. He gives praise where praise is necessary, but he also talks openly about the challenges in his own life.

7 To keep me from becoming conceited because of these surpassingly great revelations, there was given me a thorn in my flesh, a messenger of Satan, to torment me. 8 Three times I pleaded with the Lord to take it away from me. 9 But he said to me, "My grace is sufficient for you, for my power is made perfect in weakness." Therefore I will boast all the more gladly about my weaknesses, so that Christ's power may rest on me.
- 2 Corinthians 12:7-9 (NIV)

I really want to focus on the words that Paul heard from the Lord: "My grace is sufficient for you, for my power is made perfect in weakness." This is a beautiful description of God's power and grace. It doesn't require constant shows of strength and flashy displays of pride to be assigned its power; no, rather, it becomes perfected through our weakness. Paul follows that up by emphasizing that sharing weakness is not something to be ashamed of: no, rather, it is an opportunity to put Christ's strength and grace on display and allow Him to work through us as followers.

16 *Therefore, confess your sins to one another and pray for one another, that you may be healed. The prayer of a righteous person has great power as it is working.*

- James 5:16 (ESV)

This really is all just a big way to say that in order to be truly authentic and to foster authenticity in other disciples, you have to become not only comfortable with confession, but intimately familiar with it. Confession of sin is an admission of a struggle. We all struggle. Many lack this authentic accountability and become isolated in their challenge, especially when the thorn is deep in a sensitive area. That's often how we end up with leaders of the church getting caught up in traps set by the enemy. Scripture says that our adversary is prowling around like a roaring lion, seeking whom he is going to devour. The prideful inability to share our authentic challenges to God has caused even the best to stumble in isolation. God is not done with our story, just as he was not done with King David when he stumbled with Bathsheeba (see 2 Samuel 11, 12).

One of the best places to be as a Christian is to know that God already knows. He already knows your heart, the words you've said, the things you've done. He knows the same things about the people you are discipling. He is not here to condemn you, but to free you from chains of the guilt and shame. He wants you to give it all to Him. Trust that He will work through your strengths and your weaknesses. Be authentic with Him about the successes and the challenges. When your disciple shares with you their challenges just listen, do not judge. No matter how deep or long you have been in your faith, as followers, we will constantly be needing to hand things over to Christ in repentance knowing that we serve a forgiving and merciful God. Remembering that we too could stumble if we are not careful.

YOU MIGHT ASK:
What's an *authentic* struggle and success in your faith walk?

So what happens when we authentically share our success and challenges with another Christian? First of all, it bolsters our relationships. It allows you to see areas of growth in another disciple. Secondly, it keeps us in conversation with God.

[20] For where two or three are gathered together in my name, I am there among them.
- Matthew 18:20 (NIV)

A brotherly and sisterly bond forms when we confess and pray for each other. The New Testament details constantly where forgiveness occurs, there is prayer between two disciples. It also holds you, as a leader, accountable, which we discussed a bit in the earlier sections. It also helps the disciple learn to pray and listen to others in an authentic, meaningful, and grace filled way. It keeps you accountable for areas where you need to develop plans to grow in.

There hasn't been a major revival in church history without the authentic confession of sins. We must not shy away, but rather run towards Jesus; run towards community and church. Forgiveness is always found in surrendering those challenges to God and in the "one another" in scripture.

I'm not a marathon runner, but the Bible actually uses the metaphor of running a race to describe our faith throughout our lives, so it feels like a solid choice for this illustration. Runners often describe the most painful parts of the race happen as soon as they take their eyes off of the destination: their eyes off the prize, so to speak. That's when the reality of the human body hits. The climate becomes unbearable, the full-body exercise becomes laborious, and the terrain becomes sudden-ly challenging in a way that it wasn't before. Most runners are looking down when they trip and fall or slow down. Something happens psycho-logically to cause running the race to feel impossible in an instant. In our race of faith, where Jesus is at the finish line, when we look down, we're going to fall into the traps and pitfalls of sin because we took our eyes off Jesus.

[3] *You keep him in perfect peace*
whose mind is stayed on you,
because he trusts in you.

- Isaiah 26:3 (ESV)

He will give you strength when you are in need as you exercise trust. Peace comes as we focus on God and the salvation we have in Jesus who says we are forgiven! That's why it's important to have good teammates around you. They will remind you when you are authentic with your challenges. We are not meant to take this journey alone. Every pastor needs a pastor; every disciple needs to be a disciple. You give God honor when you keep your eyes on Him, and you allow Him to shine through you when you help your teammates get back up.

Sharing authentically gives us a humble and honest opportunity for repentance. When I confess my sin to a brother or sister in Christ, when I admit something, there's an opportunity for my brother or sister to say, "This is what I'm going through." The moment I say that, there is an opportunity for them to speak into my life and remind me that God is really with me and is excited to see you grow in this area. There's an opportunity for someone else to really pour into your life; to pray for you and with you. Prayer is one of the most underrated gifts God has given us as a church. I won't leave a meeting without praying for the people I'm with; we want to invite God to intercede and give another a blessing that they can't even contain.

[3] *You search out my path and my lying down*
and are acquainted with all my ways.
[4] *Even before a word is on my tongue,*

behold, O Lord, you know it all together...
⁷ Where shall I go from your Spirit?
  Or where shall I flee from your presence?

- Psalm 139:3-4, 7 (ESV)

God is so good.

On the flip side, we should be sharing and praising God for the amazing things he's doing in our lives. Success, in a spiritual sense, is also incredibly important to hear from a disciple. Sharing authentic success looks like giving praise to God. Sometimes we don't want to speak about what God is doing because we don't want to look like we're boasting. However, I believe that during the constant persecution of the early church, hearing the testimony and encouragement from Paul's letters helped the disciples welcome a new day. We may not be experiencing the same level of persecution, but sharing our praise to God for what he's doing in our lives is a hope-filled reminder that God is still at work. If we know that God is never going to leave and forsake us, there has to be some semblance of truth to Him responding in our world. He is not a God that lives in some far-off distance or keeps us at arm's length. He is here. Now. God is here helping my neighbor and friends, that my turn is coming. When David said in Psalm 27:13, "I believe that I shall look upon the goodness of the LORD in the land of the living!" He was not wrong!

How can we consider stirring up one another through love and good works if we're never real with each other? If we never meet with one another? If we never encourage one another? If we can never mourn with each other?

You should ask yourself:
- Am I being authentic with God about my challenges and sin?
- Am I being real and authentic about my struggles with another in the faith?
- Am I approachable and forgiving when others share authentically with me?

How in the Christian faith can I encourage someone? I can encourage someone by sharing some of the things that the Lord is doing in my life. I can share a story of someone coming to faith. I can be there for someone who is feeling crushed, joyless, and outcast like David did after he sinned with Bathsheba. This part of the relationship takes a while to develop. But when it is, our eyes remain focused on Jesus at the finish line of our faith.

R: REACH

¹⁸ *And Jesus came and said to them, "All authority in heaven and on earth has been given to me.* ¹⁹ *Go therefore and make disciples of all nations, baptizing them in the name of the Father and of the Son and of the Holy Spirit,* ²⁰ *teaching them to observe all that I have commanded you. And behold, I am with you always, to the end of the age."*

- Matthew 28:18-20 (ESV)

We've looked at discipleship now from a lot of angles, all of which involve truly hearing another person. *HIS WORD* gave us what we base our discipleship on. *ENGAGE* encourages us to ask God how He will use our gifts, talents, and abilities. *AUTHENTICITY* reminds us why listening and sharing matter so much. Now, we're going to look at how reaching others calls on us to ask who and where we are called to disciple next. God's heart is for the Lost. Our job is to be ambassadors. Christianity has always spread through new people and places through the multiplication of disciples.

The reality is this: as of March 2020 there are roughly 7.8 billion people on the planet, and thousands of those people groups that need to be reached. A 2015 Pew Research study found that in the United States alone, the number of religiously unaffiliated adults has increased by roughly 19 million since 2007. There are now roughly 56 million religiously unaffiliated adults in the U.S.

Reaching is, like everything else in discipleship, a measure of trust. It reminds us, often in the most concrete way, how much we have left to grow or how far we have come in trusting God completely and wholly. This point is entirely about who we are reaching today or tomorrow. It looks like specifically asking God to bring someone into your life or bring you to a place that you need to be sharing Him with. It could be someone as familiar as a family member, coworker, or neighbor. It could be someone as distant as a stranger you meet on the train. This is asking the Lord to intervene in the process of the work that He has called us to do; impacting our world, but asking God to give us the strength to do it and the wisdom to follow to the places He wants us to be at. If you're not thinking about 'who' or 'where,' to go and spread the gospel next, you aren't really there yet, per se, as a leader or a disciple.

It's a truly powerful exercise of faith and an amazing opportunity to watch God change someone and see His power through them. If a disciple, church, network is praying specifically and fervently for people or zip codes, amazing things can happen! We are instruments for God's glory, which makes this part of discipleship truly exciting.

YOU MIGHT ASK:
Who or where do you want to reach?

There are two important reminders that this question offers to a disciple. The first one is the mission, which Jesus gives very directly in Matthew 28. By asking this question of who or where to reach next with someone, it allows the disciple to be reminded of the Great Commission where Jesus called us to go. Pray that God will place someone in your life that you can share life with and share Christ with. This question places an action step to accountability with one another. Our faith in God and obedience to His Word stir our hearts to share Jesus with others.

[8] But you will receive power when the Holy Spirit has come upon you; and you shall be My witnesses both in Jerusalem, and in all Judea and Samaria, and even to the remotest part of the earth.

- Acts 1:8 (NASB)

My good friends Paul and Theresa Root absolutely love mangoes. The Philippines has some of the best. When Paul and I traveled to the Philippines to be a part of a Converge church planting conference, I lost count of how many times he told me he loved mangoes. At the conference, we saw God move in a mighty way. On the final day of the conference, leader after leader prayerfully responded to the call to reach the lost for Christ. They committed to sending out planters and making disciples. It is the call of every Christian. Just like a mango. In the grand scheme of it all (Paul won't like this), a mango's job isn't to be a sweet and refreshing fruit. Its purpose is to make more mango trees! Similarly, our purpose is not just to be consumers of the faith. It is to make disciples!

We are not meant to hide behind big desks and social media posts. Reaching is an action, it requires your hands and feet, as it requires the hands and feet of the church to reach its community. Faith is an inward change producing outward responses. The prayer declares that we are not called to just sit around and know lots of cool Bible things, it is to go and intentionally make disciples!

The second reminder is that it puts the prayer emphasis on the lost. In Luke 14:15-24, Jesus tells the Parable of the Great Banquet. He tells of a man who invites friends to a banquet, and when they all have excuses as to why they can't show, the master of the house sends a servant to go fetch the socially outcast, the hungry, the poor, and they share in his banquet with him. Jesus uses this illustration as another reminder to His disciples that there is no one unworthy to hear the gospel and accept it, nor is there a person He can't seek out. In the very next chapter Jesus gives another parable featuring a lost sheep.

4 *What man of you, having a hundred sheep, if he has lost one of them, does not leave the ninety-nine in the open country, and go after the one that is lost, until he finds it?*

- Luke 15:4 (ESV)

God goes to extraordinary lengths to rescue the lost. He goes so far as to leave 99 sheep to save the lost one. It's easy for us to think, "Relax here Jesus, we have enough... there's no need to risk any more resources or even your life for one lamb that has wandered off." But the Good Shepherd knows and loves that one lost lamb better than anyone ever will with priceless love. His heart is to find that lost lamb.

⁵ When he has found it, he lays it on his shoulders, rejoicing. ⁶ And when he comes home, he calls together his friends and his neighbors, saying to them, 'Rejoice with me, for I have found my sheep which was lost!'
- Luke 15:5-6 (NASB)

This prayerful question reminds us that we are a part of the celebration when even one is rescued!

²¹ So Jesus said to them again, "Peace be with you; as the Father has sent Me, I also send you."
- John 20:21 (NASB)

Reaching is a workout, an exercise of what we have been feeding on. It's the call from God to multiply. He wants us to walk in our faith, not just stand around, stagnant in it. Ask God to send us. Not somebody else. Me. You. The person you are walking the H.E.A.R. starting point of discipleship method with.

You should ask yourself:
- Who is in my sphere of influence that is far from God?
- Where are the neighborhoods or language barriers that our church or churches are not yet reaching?
- Does my heart break for the lost in my city?

This is usually one of the shorter question responses that you will have out of the four with God and from your disciple. The list of people and places to reach may stay the same for days, weeks, months, or longer. Keep praying and watch what the Lord does!

God is so good.

May He grant us the strength we need to be His hands and feet. And multiply.

AFTERWORD

Like I said in the beginning, we live in a loud world. A world full of distractions that can easily distract us from the mission of God. Jesus has commanded us to make disciples. However, all too often, we end up repelling people. Every generation has had struggles with reaching the next one. The next generation especially needs to be heard and need to hear from God.

I remember teaching the H.E.A.R. method at a church, and there was one 19-year-old lady sitting by herself. Being an old millennial, I asked the older generation in the room what they thought was the best way to have a conversation with the millennial generation (born 1981 to 1996). The older voices in the room began to chuckle. They agreed that texting or social media was the preferred method of conversation for that generation. They made a few other poking fun remarks about the next generation, like the generation before them did with them.

However, their mouths dropped when I told them that the best method of conversation is face to face. Then, like many before her, the 19-year-old began nodding her head in agreement while they all wrestled with their assumptions.

Let's deploy this method and begin to raise up our next generations. Let's move into some deeper conversations. The times we live in allow this to be possible since most small talk about what is going on in someone's life is already online. So let's shut up and shema once again.

I pray that this simple starting point method of discipleship can bless your walk with God and your discipleship relationships.

Let's listen and obey. Now go, make disciples of Christ!

- CHRIS LOVELACE

WORKBOOK

INSTRUCTIONS FOR ONE ON ONE DISCIPLESHIP ACCOUNTABILITY SESSIONS:

1. Start the formal discipleship time with H question.
2. Train the disciple to ask you the same question.
3. Ask a follow up E.A.R. question.
4. Repeat steps 2 and 3 as your time permits.
5. Pray for each other.

INSTRUCTIONS FOR PERSONAL DEVOTION:

1. Select passage from your Bible Devotion/Study/Sermon & Journal what you H.E.A.R. on the following pages.
2. Pray.

QUICK ONE-ON-ONE DISCIPLESHIP TIPS:

- There there's no such thing as a wrong answer.
- Do not interrupt, correct, display disapproval when your disciple is sharing.
- Focus on your disciple, listening to the answer as if a quiz is coming after and your life depended on you getting a good grade!
- You don't have to ask every question in one sitting, but always ask the H and make sure to get to the ones you missed next time.
- You don't have to phrase the question the same way I have (get creative over time, make it your own!).
- Be authentic, be humble, be real.
- To go deeper, pair with a Bible study of your choice!
- Remember to celebrate!

JOURNAL

H – HIS WORD: WHAT IS GOD SAYING TO YOU IN HIS WORD?

JOURNAL

E – ENGAGE: WHO ARE YOU ENGAGING WITH YOUR TIME, TREASURE, AND TALENT?

JOURNAL

A – AUTHENTIC: WHAT'S AN AUTHENTIC STRUGGLE AND SUCCESS IN YOUR FAITH WALK?

_____

_____

_____

_____

_____

_____

_____

_____

_____

_____

_____

_____

_____

_____

_____

_____

_____

_____

_____

_____

_____

_____

_____

_____

_____

JOURNAL

R – REACH: WHO OR WHERE DO YOU WANT TO REACH?

_____
_____
_____
_____
_____
_____
_____
_____
_____
_____
_____
_____
_____
_____
_____
_____
_____
_____
_____
_____
_____
_____
_____
_____

JOURNAL

R – REACH: WHO OR WHERE DO YOU WANT TO REACH?

NOTES

CPSIA information can be obtained
at www.ICGtesting.com
Printed in the USA
BVHW071317131021
618855BV00003B/404